MW01200889

what
now?

what
now?

A college student's guide to continued catholic faith

Jennifer Redenius

What Now? A College Student's Guide to Continued Catholic Faith. Copyright © 2017 by Jennifer Redenius. All rights reserved. No part of this book may be used or reproduced in any manner whatsoever without written permission from the author, except in the case of brief quotations embodied in critical articles or reviews.

ISBN: 978-0-9983058-3-7

Published and printed in the United States of America by the Write Place, Inc. For more information, please contact:

the Write Place, Inc.
809 W. 8th Street, Suite 2
Pella, Iowa 50219
www.thewriteplace.biz

Cover design by Chris Handlos and interior design by Michelle Stam, the Write Place, Inc.

Copies of this book may be ordered online at the Write Place website, Amazon, and BarnesandNoble.com.

Dedication

To Jeff, for encouraging me to do this.

Prayer of Saint Thomas Aquinas
(A Student's Prayer)

Come, Holy Spirit, Divine Creator, true source of light and fountain of wisdom! Pour forth your brilliance upon my dense intellect, dissipate the darkness which covers me, that of sin and of ignorance. Grant me a penetrating mind to understand, a retentive memory, method, and ease in learning, the lucidity to comprehend, and abundant grace in expressing myself. Guide the beginning of my work, direct its progress, and bring it to successful completion. This I ask through Jesus Christ, true God and true man, living and reigning with You and the Father, forever and ever. Amen.

Table of Contents

Preface

Congratulations on getting to the point in life when you are preparing to leave, or have already left, the family nest! This exciting time is bound to bring many changes with it as you embark on new adventures.

The idea for this book came to me as I was reflecting on my own transition to adulthood. After leaving home, I quickly discovered the exhausting number of choices and decisions I would soon have to make. Some of these were small choices, while other decisions weighed heavily on the path of my future. It wasn't long after I thought I had made the transition to adulthood that I realized my journey wasn't even close to being finished. I needed to continually rely on my faith in each new chapter of my life. It is my hope that through this book I will provide you with a real, honest toolkit to help ease your transition to adulthood. I'm sure you, too, will discover there is much more to adulthood than no curfew and an unlimited number of frozen pizza suppers.

While one era of your story may be coming to a close now, a whole new adventure awaits you. Each section of this book is centered on my first week away from home. In each section, I'll pose a challenge I advise you to take on as you embark on your journey to adulthood. I hope these challenges make the transition a bit easier for you and that you find the value in growing in your Catholic faith as you continue to mature. Thank you for allowing me to accompany you on this journey!

Part One

Friday: Finding Yourself Away From Home

"Trust in the Lord with all your heart and lean not on your own understanding; in all your ways submit to him, and he will make your paths straight." (Proverbs 3:5-6)

"So, what are your future plans?"

It was August 2008, and I was an itty-bitty little freshman at the University of Iowa. As I prepared to step out of my parents' vehicle and into my new dorm, I was asked the above question (for the hundredth time) by the campus guide who was showing me to my room. At the time, my bold 17-year-old self thought she knew exactly what she was going to do. My plans were to attend the University of Iowa and attain a degree in journalism. After being raised in a small Midwestern town of around 2,000 people, I was ready to branch out, make new friends, and surround myself with a new culture. I was incredibly excited to leave home and be on my own for the first time. No rules. No curfew. No vegetables at supper if I didn't want them. I was free! Life was going to be blissful.

And then my parents drove off and left me there.

Suddenly, I was not so sure of my plans. As I stood there, facing the giant brick building that was going to be my home for the next year, I faced the first of many decisions I was about to make as an adult: Who did I want to be? Without my parents there to tell me what to do or how to act, who did I want to become?

In retrospect, I probably only stood there looking utterly lost for a second or two. For me, though, that moment of reflection lasted much longer. That moment before I walked into my new future has stuck with me to this day.

The beauty of leaving home and starting a new chapter is you get the choice to be whomever you want to be. While my upbringing played a large role in developing my morals, beliefs, and priorities, I was about to *choose* if I wanted to continue on that path. You may be in a similar situation. You, too, will get the opportunity to choose which path to take. You get to choose who you want to become.

As I walked away from my parents' vehicle, I started second-guessing myself. *Am I meant to be here? Do I really want to be a journalist? How am I going to get along with my new roommate?* As the doubts started rolling in, I made a conscious decision to turn my fears over to God. Standing there fretting about it was going to get me nowhere. I didn't have my parents to turn to. I didn't have my friends to turn to—I hadn't even met anyone on campus yet! I had no one to turn to except God, so in that moment, I had to trust He knew the right plan for me. I said a silent prayer in which I asked for guidance, and with that, I entered my dorm room for the first time, ready to begin my new chapter.

I credit that conscious decision to turn my doubts over to God as the main reason I, unlike so many of my peers, continued to grow in my Catholic faith throughout college. That one silent prayer turned into a habit of prayer throughout the next few years. That one decision made an immeasurable difference in my life.

I am extremely lucky this moment of reflection and decision happened so quickly after leaving home. Shoot, I had not even been on campus for more than a half hour before I figured out I needed to turn my doubts and fears to God because He would be there to listen. While it may not happen as quickly for you, I encourage you to learn from my experience.

And what a great opportunity to present my first challenge to you: **When you find yourself away from home for the first time and on the path to adulthood, prepare as much as you can. But when the time comes to step up to the plate and begin your adventure, turn your doubts to God.**

Challenge # 1

When you find yourself away from home for the first time and on the path to adulthood, prepare as much as you can. But when the time comes to step up to the plate and begin your adventure, turn your doubts to God.

We all want to know our purpose in life. We want to know why we were created, what we are meant to do, how we are supposed to act. The culture we live in puts a lot of emphasis on what we do with our time. So much of what we "do" defines who we are. Every question we ask, every hope we have, every goal we seek to accomplish must come first from our personal relationship with God.

As you prepare to find yourself away from home for the first time, you may visualize yourself as a lone body standing in front of 100 different paths to choose from. I'm not just talking about schooling or career choices. I am talking about friendships you'll choose to make, clubs you'll choose to join, activities you'll choose to participate in, how you'll choose to spend your free time. Whether you listen to Robert Frost and take the road not taken is up to you, but I do hope that as you stare out at these paths ahead, you seek first your relationship with God. When you do this, it becomes easier to choose a path because you're trusting that through your relationship with Him, you will go in the right direction.

Imagine a life where your relationship with God determines everything else in your life. Imagine you are not motivated by social status, money,

Instagram followers, or external rewards. What would that life look like for you? Seriously, think about it!

Here are my top three suggestions to help you remember God is directing your path, and as long as you put your relationship with Him first, you will be headed in the right direction.

1. **Prepare.** Do your research. While you need to put your relationship with God first, you need to take care of yourself, too. God will not miraculously put a career path at your doorstep. Go on college visits. Ask mentors for their advice. Save up your money. Read, read, and read some more. Make sure you explore all the possibilities God has given to you. And when it comes time to leave home, make sure you pack enough clothes, plenty of snacks, your Bible, and a toothbrush!

2. **Self-Reflect.** Take some time each day to reflect on who you are and who you want to be. If you don't know who or what you want to be the moment you leave home, that is OKAY! The beauty of the life God has given you is that you have free will to decide and learn as you go. No growth will take place without self-reflection, though. Make a point each day, or even each week, to reflect on who you're becoming and if the path you're going down is the one you actually want to follow.

3. **Pray.** This is obviously the most important of the three. If your relationship with God is going to direct the rest of your decisions, you need to pray and talk with Him about His plans for you. Here is a hint: You will NEVER be fully prepared to find yourself away from home for the first time. You will never have reflected enough to be 100% sure of who and what you want to be. You will always forget to buy or bring a necessity. This is where prayer comes in. Turn your doubts over to God, and He will show you the right path to take. Be flexible and open to change, and don't get down on yourself if you don't have it all figured out right away.

Remember my challenge for this section as well: **When you find yourself away from home for the first time and on the path to adulthood, prepare as much as you can. But when the time comes to step up to the plate and begin your adventure, turn your doubts to God.**

Prayer to reflect on:

God, I have prepared. I am ready to embark on my new journey. Please watch over me as I begin this new adventure in my life. Help me to remember that my relationship with You is most important and that if I keep that in mind, I will be okay. Help me to do what I need to do to best fulfill Your plans for me. Guide my decision-making so I choose the best plan for me. Thank you for giving me this opportunity to embark on a new journey. Help me remember that Your plan for me is so much larger than my own. Amen.

Part Two

Saturday:
Finding Faith

"Consequently, faith comes from hearing the message, and the message is heard through the word about Christ."
(Romans 10:17)

It didn't take longer than one day on campus for me to realize I had a lot to learn. The itty-bitty little freshman quickly realized that if she continued to walk to class, she had to buy better shoes than flip-flop sandals. I realized that putting sheets on a lofted bed was much harder than I'd thought it would be. I realized that if I continued to eat the ice cream at lunch and supper, I would soon gain the "freshman fifteen." I realized that, no, Jenny, you cannot just get on any campus bus and assume it will take you where you need to go. I also realized it was going to be very, very easy to surround myself with the wrong things and wrong people—they were everywhere!

Because my first day on campus was a Friday, I was lucky enough to have a weekend to adjust before I began my coursework the following Monday. I had survived my first night away, and I woke up Saturday eager to explore my new surroundings and meet new people. It was during this venture to meet new people that I made the second major decision that impacted my future as a young Catholic. Remember, my first major decision was turning my doubts over to God. My second decision came when a girl who lived across the hall asked if I wanted to attend Mass with her that Saturday evening. Normally, I would have agreed, but I had already been asked to go out to supper with a few other girls living on my floor. I had a decision to make. I realized that during my never-ending preparations for college, I'd forgotten to research what church I wanted to attend...and if I even wanted to attend. With my newfound freedom came the choice of possibly skipping weekend Mass. I no longer had my parents telling me to go, and I had been so consumed with thinking about how I was going to fit all of my stuff into a tiny dorm room that I'd forgotten to even think about where to attend church.

When the girl asked me to go to Mass with her, I paused, not knowing what to do. *Do I go out with all my new friends, or do I attend Mass with this girl I don't really know?*

I decided it would be worth it to at least try out a church in my new town, so I made the decision to attend Mass and then meet up with my friends after. I had known from the start that I didn't want to surround myself with the wrong crowd, and I figured that this girl who was asking me to attend Mass with her would probably be a good friend to make. We walked over to the church together, and I remember walking into the sanctuary and feeling right at home.

The beauty of the Catholic Mass is that no matter where you are, the process of Mass is the same. After experiencing 48 hours of culture shock, I felt like I was back home. I got back into my routine of talking to God, singing my favorite hymns, and interacting with the Gospel. Not only did I feel like I was back at home, I realized how many other students were at Mass with me. I very quickly realized that if I wanted to find a group of friends that also placed their relationship with God first, I should start here. Looking back, I am so thankful I was asked to go to Mass that day. While I assume I would have eventually found my way to a church while at college, who knows how long it would have taken me to give up social outings to attend Mass on the weekend!

And here comes my second challenge to you: **Make a point to attend Mass starting week one.** It is only an hour of your time. It will allow you to take a step back once a week and reevaluate where you're at on the path you started out on when you left

home. Make a conscious decision to make it a habit from the get-go. Don't put off finding a church home until later on. If you make an effort from week one, you are more likely to continue the habit.

You may not be as lucky as I was in that I had a friend ask me to attend Mass with her. Regardless, I challenge you to go to Mass, even if you go alone. I promise you will quickly make friends. And even if you do go alone, use it as a time for individual, personal reflection.

To be totally transparent, when you leave home, you will be bombarded with different ways to spend your time. Partying will become a more realistic opportunity. Social engagements will become more of a priority. Studying (hopefully) will become a high priority on your list if you choose to pursue higher education. You may work a job that requires much of your time and energy. You, just like me, will have to make a decision. Will you attend Mass, or will you choose to spend that hour each week in a different way? Believe me, God WANTS you to enjoy life. He wants you to go have fun with friends. He wants to you find a meaningful career. He wants you to sleep in on the weekends if that is what you need. But He also wants you to seek a closer relationship with Him. He wants you to find your faith.

Here is a little secret: It is REALLY hard to find your faith if you do not attend Mass.

And please, don't go to Mass simply because your parents always made you go or because I am telling you to go. Go to Mass because you WANT to be there. Go because you WANT to find your faith and grow closer to God. Think of what Matthew 18:20 says: "For where two or three gather in my name, there am I with them." Going to Mass is another way for you to interact with God.

I cannot lie; giving up social obligations or setting an early alarm on Sunday was a difficult choice to make at times. But no matter what, I always made the effort to go. I encourage you to do the same and allot time for Mass each week, starting week one. It will be easier for you to find your faith after you leave home if you actively seek it out. You cannot find what you are not searching for. Imagine what life would look like if you made a conscious decision to find your faith by actively participating in Mass once a week. Imagine how much your relationship with God would grow.

As you prepare to find your faith at this new stage in your life, here are my top three suggestions for discovering the beauty of keeping the Catholic faith in your life:

1. **Set a goal to continue your faith journey and stick to it.** Learn from my mistake. I was so consumed with preparing for the logistics of leaving home that I did not make a point to set a goal of finding my faith while out on my own. I made no effort to research different churches in the area, and while I had packed my Bible, I was more concerned with packing enough Hawkeye attire to wear on game days. As you prepare to leave home, make it a goal to find your faith as you seek to find yourself. You will soon discover the two are interconnected. Make an effort to read the Bible frequently. Even if it is just a verse. It literally is the Word of God. If you want advice on how to live your life, I suggest looking directly at the Word of God for direction. You are more likely to follow through on something if you make it a goal, so set high standards for yourself. Seek out your faith as you go through this process of growing up.

2. **Get involved with Mass.** Step one of finding your faith, as stated above, is simply making an effort to attend Mass on a weekly basis. Step two is to become an active participant in Mass. For starters, try actively paying attention as opposed to silently quizzing yourself over biology terms during the homily. Once you've mastered the art of focusing on the Mass, try bringing a friend. Imagine how beautiful and faith-filled our world would be if every student reached out and invited one friend to Mass.

3. **Pray.** Recognize this one? It's going to be hard for you to find your faith if you don't make an effort to pray every day. Talk to God. Tell Him your worries and fears. Tell him your triumphs. God WANTS a relationship with you. He WANTS you to pursue your faith. Make daily prayer part of the goal you set for yourself. Whether it's on the drive to work, during your walk to class, or before you go to bed at night, make an effort to talk with God every day—believe me, He is there listening.

Remember my challenge for this section as well: **Make a point to attend Mass starting week one.** Set a goal to find your faith and actively put forth an effort to do so through daily prayer and weekly Mass. I personally made an effort each week to attend Mass, and it got me through college and has gotten me through my adventures since then. Mass gave me reprieve when I was stressed about a final exam or about a job. It gave me an outlet to express my love of God. It brought so many friendships to my life. I am still growing and finding my faith, but making the decision to attend Mass and pray every day has made all the difference.

Prayer to reflect on:

As I embark on this new adventure, God, please help me to continue to find my faith. Help me set goals for myself and attain them. It is my choice, God, to further build my relationship with You. When I am tempted to put other things first, help me remember the importance of finding and building my faith in You. Thank you for this opportunity to go out on my own for the first time. Guide me to find my faith in You each day. Amen.

Part Three

Monday: Finding Purpose

"He has saved us and called us to a holy life—not because of any-thing we have done but because of his own purpose and grace."
(2 Timothy 1:9)

Life is meant to be lived with purpose, direction, and meaning. We all tend to wish for the same things in life: happiness, joy, love, success, and purpose. At some point in all of our lives, we ask, "Why am I here? What is my purpose? What am I meant to do?" We ask these questions because deep in our hearts, we know there is an answer for them. I am sure that as you prepared to leave home, you asked some of these same questions.

The reality is that we (myself included) often look for the answers to these questions in the wrong places. We seek answers to these questions in places that will not always result in happiness, joy, love, or success.

After I survived the first weekend away from home, it was time for the first week of classes. It was Monday, and I had made it through my first two classes of the day. I decided to take an afternoon break at a local coffee shop, as I'd always wanted to live out the college ideal of sitting in a coffee shop on a rainy afternoon, looking scholarly with all of my books.

I'm not sure how well I fit into that mold, because instead of looking like a scholarly college student, I'm sure I came across as frazzled, nervous, and overwhelmed.

I ordered my steamy mocha latte and sat down at a table to begin working on the assignments that had already been given to me. I wasn't used to being assigned so much work on the first day. Wasn't the first day just about going over the syllabus? For the life of me, I couldn't concentrate on my studies. The only thing I could think about was how long the next four years were going to be. I could not imagine being so passionate about something that it would be worth devoting all my time and energy to it for the next four years. I began second-guessing my major of choice. I began second-guessing my decision to go to college at all.

Yes, I was aware I was not meant to live my life by sitting in coffee shops, appearing to be scholarly, while looking and feeling utterly confused.

So, what was I supposed to be doing?

It was at that point I realized I had been searching for my purpose in all the wrong places. I really needed to reevaluate my plans.

When deciding my future plans as a high school senior, I had thought about how much money I would make in each career choice. I had thought about what type of career would lend itself well to having a family someday. I had thought about what my friends and family would think of my decision. I'd decided to go to college because I was never really given a different choice.

At no point had I considered what God had planned for me. I was seeking to find my purpose from external factors that wouldn't necessarily result in happiness.

Did I have some divine intervention at that point while drinking my mocha latte, a sudden realization of exactly what I was meant to be doing?

No.

But it was at that point that I started to pray about it. I started to talk to God about my reservations and fears about the future. I prayed about my hopes for the future. I asked God to help me find my purpose in life. I stopped thinking about how my family and friends might view my future plans, and instead, I thought about what God would want for me.

When I let go of my fears and started asking God for guidance, I realized everything was going to be okay. I realized that once I found a subject area I was truly passionate about, I would love school and love learning more about it. In hindsight, that is exactly what happened. I tried out many different courses until I found something I really loved, and then I pursued that interest with grit, hard work, and passion.

That Monday was another turning point for me. Even though I'd turned my doubts to God when I first arrived on campus, and even though I'd begun to find my faith by attending Mass and setting a goal of praying frequently, up until that point, I hadn't sought to find my purpose through God. When I made that decision, I felt a sense of peace. Yes, I had hundreds of career paths to choose from, but at that point, I began to trust God would help me navigate my options.

Even today, I still ask, "Why am I here?" I still seek to find my purpose because, in my experience, it is an ongoing path to discovery. As you grow, mature, and learn more, your passions change and your purpose in life evolves. You may never find one specific area or thing that becomes your "purpose," but as you grow and learn more about yourself and your faith, I hope you ask God to help you along the road to finding out why you are here. Imagine what your life would be like if you trusted that God has a plan for you and that someday you will discover what it is.

And while you explore who you are meant to be, what you are meant to do, and who you are meant to be with, I challenge you to always remember what your real purpose is (and here comes challenge number three): **Always remember that your number-one purpose in life is to love God and show His love to others**. God has called you to a holy, loving life. Not because of some specific gift YOU have. Rather, He has called you to a holy, loving life because of what He gave us—His Son. At the end of the day, if you make a point to love God

Challenge # 3

Always remember that your number-one purpose in life is to love God and show His love to others.

and show His love to others, you are serving your main purpose. Imagine if everyone in this world made loving God and loving others their primary purpose in life. How different would our world look?

Depending on where you are in your journey, you may have already decided on a career path. Or, you may be just starting to figure it out. You may have no idea where to start. I challenge you to first remember that your purpose every day when you wake up is to love God and show His love to others. Second, I challenge you to pray about it. Even when you think you've figured it out, continue to seek God's guidance because you will always be working to discover your purpose. Find what you love doing, and then find a way to make a living from it.

In your first week or month away from home, you may have an experience similar to the one I had. You may question your purpose in life, and you may question if what you signed up for is what you are actually meant to do. I have had many friends and family members go through the same thing. On the first day my husband began graduate school to become a Doctor of Chiropractic, he called me in tears (yes, full-fledged tears), wondering if he had made the right decision—knowing full well the stressors that would come with four years of graduate school. The idea of four years of graduate school was incredibly daunting for both of us. I told him the same thing I am telling you: Trust that God is leading you on the right path to finding your purpose. If you pray about it, God will help you figure out what you are supposed to be doing.

As you begin to consider your future plans, or as you reevaluate what your purpose is, I encourage you to take these suggestions into consideration:

1. **Stop looking in the wrong places.** When you seek to find your purpose, avoid looking in the wrong places. Do not focus on which option will bring you the most money. Do not focus on which option will please your family members or friends. Do not focus on which option will bring immediate satisfaction. Instead, reflect on what your personal strengths are. Reflect on what God might be calling you to do. Reflect on what you love doing and how you could make a career out of it. As you

reflect on these things, be open to changing your plans. If your original plan isn't leaving you feeling fulfilled, it may be time to reevaluate.

2. **Work hard.** God will not magically throw your purpose in life directly in your lap. You need to work to find it. Study hard. Work hard. Promise yourself that no job will ever be "beneath" you because each job you have is a stepping stone to the next one. God will help you while you help yourself. As you embark on your new adventure, make a promise that you will work hard at everything you do because you will not find your passion by putting forth half your potential effort. Think of Colossians 3:23. It says, "Whatever you do, work at it with all your heart, as working for the Lord, not for human masters." Act as if every job you have will bring you closer to the purpose God has planned for you. Not every day in your pursuit to find your purpose will be a great day. You may have a difficult exam, or you may have to work a job you aren't thrilled about. There will undoubtedly be setbacks. Remember, though, that God rewards hard work. Put in the effort needed to find your purpose, and God will help you along the way.

3. **Pray.** Do you see a theme? As with the other sections in this book, payer is the most important suggestion I have for you here. As you work hard at whatever you're doing, make a point to pray about it. Ask God for His guidance in finding your passion and purpose in life. Continually reflect on your own strengths and your own happiness. Are you feeling fulfilled by what you are doing? If not, ask God to help you find a purpose that leaves you feeling fulfilled. When in doubt, turn your questions to God.

Remember my challenge for this section as well: **Always remember that your number-one purpose in life is to love God and show His love to others.** Remember that God has called you to a holy, loving life. At the end of the day, if you have done that, then you are fulfilling God's primary purpose for you.

Prayer to reflect on:

In the coming days, months, and years, God, I ask You to help me find my purpose in life. Help me to remember that if I am loving You and showing Your love to others, I will be serving Your number-one purpose for me. As I navigate my future, help me to find a purpose that leads me to feeling fulfilled. Thank you for giving me the free will to make my own decisions about my life. Please help me to make decisions that will allow me to find my purpose. Amen.

Part Four

Wednesday: Finding Direction

"Whether you turn to the right or to the left, your ears will hear a voice behind you, saying, 'This is the way; walk in it.'" (Isaiah: 30:2)

In the first section of this book, I told you that at some point, you will find yourself a lone body standing in front of 100 paths. When given all these options, you will find yourself seeking guidance on which direction to go.

While there are many similarities between finding your purpose and finding your direction, there is a very distinct difference between the two. Finding your purpose is a lot like setting a long-term goal. What are you working towards? Who do you want to become? Once you have figured that out (even if you have just begun reflecting on it), the next step is deciding which direction to take to get you to that goal. What steps do you need to take? Which route should you travel?

Every aspect of your life is a direct result of the choices you make. One wrong choice can impact you and your future in more ways than one. I promise you that every single day you will be bombarded with choices. Your future will be a product of how you act upon those choices. Think about how often you hit the snooze button, for example. What would your life be like if you actively embraced each new day or opportunity as opposed to hitting snooze over and over again?

Each decision you make, no matter how big or small, will create a habit for handling future decisions. It is in your best interest to ask God to guide you through each major decision you need to make. If you are in a position where you're faced with many different options, ask God to assist you in navigating which path to take.

This idea was made clear to me soon after I left home. It was the Wednesday of my first week of college, and it was the first time I had the opportunity to meet with my academic advisor. Right away, my advisor began talking to me about what the next four years would look like. She put a document in front of me that was filled with slots for courses for the next four years of my life. As I looked at the sheet in front of me, my advisor began explaining that the goal of this sheet was to help outline and plan the next four years so I could graduate on time and with enough credits to earn a degree. She began discussing all the different options I had in regards to courses and which options would land me with a certain degree or minor in a subject area. Needless to say, I became very overwhelmed.

If I took one path, I would be taking on more semester hours each term than I had originally planned to. But if I did that, I could also attain a minor along with my bachelor's degree. If I took a different path, I wouldn't necessarily get a minor, but I wouldn't be taking as many semester hours of coursework. I was lost. I had no idea which route to go. I knew my strengths and weaknesses, and I thought I knew how to turn those into a career plan. However, I had no idea which route I should take to get there. I think my advisor sensed my uncertainty because she allowed me to take the planning sheet home and sign up to visit her a week later to go over the decisions I made.

I left that office feeling totally lost. The courses I would write down on that sheet of paper would dramatically impact my future. I had left home less than a week ago. In my mind, I was not ready to make such a big decision entirely on my own!

It was at that point I made another realization that has greatly impacted my life. I realized that whatever path I chose, it was going to be okay as long as I looked to God for direction. As long as I was not being motivated by the wrong things (what would be the easier choice, what would result in more money, what would be the more popular option), I would be headed in the right direction. The passage from the Bible I quoted at the beginning of this section speaks loudly to this fact. As long as you are looking to God for direction, no matter which path you choose, you will have chosen the right one.

This brings me to my next challenge for you: **Do not stress out too much about the decisions you will have to make. As long as you are being motivated by the right things, and as long as you are making it your priority to love God and show His love to others, you will be okay.** In retrospect, I'm sure you will find that you would do some things differently if you could. However, God has a plan for you, and if you seek His council when making these decisions, you will be headed in the right direction. It will be okay!

When you are in a position where you need to make a difficult decision, reflect on Proverbs 3:5, which says, "Trust in the Lord with all your heart and lean not on your own understanding." Do your research. Self-reflect. Examine all of your options closely. Keep in mind, though, that no matter how much you research, self-reflect, or look into your options, you will never know what God knows. You MUST ask for His guidance.

When I look back on that Wednesday, I laugh because in reality, that one sheet of paper did not dictate my next four years. It

---

Challenge # 4

Do not stress out too much about the decisions you will have to make. As long as you are being motivated by the right things, and as long as you are making it your priority to love God and show His love to others, you will be okay.

actually turned out that I went down a variety of paths. I changed majors and enrolled in new courses more than once in those four years. I became involved with clubs, volunteering opportunities, and campus organizations that all shaped my final decision on what degree I wanted to graduate with. Looking back, I discovered that the road I took to get to where I am today was multi-faceted, curvy, and sometimes even backwards. No matter which direction I took, though, God was there with me, directing me on which way to go. Would I go back and do some things differently? Sure! However, I would not trade my experiences and the decisions I made for anything because they have gotten me to where I am today. They have made me the person I am today.

Take a moment to reflect on where you are today. How many different decisions have you made or have your parents/guardians made for you that have altered the path you took to get to where you are right now? You may find comfort in reflecting on how many decisions you've already made in order to get to where you are today. You may also find that with each decision you made, God was with you, whether you realized it or not.

We all desire direction in our lives. We want to know where we are going. We want to be able to see what we're supposed to be doing and how we're supposed to get there. Our lives are meant to be directed by God. He is the one who will give you direction in life. However, you are not a puppet of God. He gave you the gift of free will. Regardless of what you choose, God will never abandon you. He will always be there to guide you on whichever path you decide to take.

And I'm not just talking about career choices or schooling choices. You will be confronted with decisions in all aspects of your life. How will you spend your evenings? Which clubs will you join? Who will you spend your time with? The list of decisions you'll make that will impact your future goes on and on.

As you begin to navigate which direction you should go or which decision you should make, I encourage you to follow these three suggestions:

1. **Assess all of your options**. When you are at a crossroads or a point in your life when you need to decide which path to take, do not make a

hasty decision. Consider your options. Weigh the pros and cons. As you assess your options, though, make sure you're taking the right things into consideration. Do not be persuaded by which option will bring you more money, which option will bring you the greatest number of Facebook "likes," which option will be the easiest or result in short-term success, or which option will be most popular with others. Rather, when you are confronted with the many roads you could take, think about which road will bring you the most long-term happiness. Think about which road will lead most directly to your goal. Consider which option will allow you to keep your number-one purpose at heart: showing love to God and showing His love to others.

2. **Reflect on what is motivating you.** As you are faced with choosing a path, you may find it helpful to think about what is driving you. Are your parents or guardians motivating you? Is money motivating you? Is popularity motivating you? Are you motivated by extrinsic rewards? If you're being motivated by the wrong things, you may find yourself going in a direction you may not want to go. When the factors that motivate you align with the plan God has created just for you, it becomes easier to decide which path to take.

3. **Pray.** I am hoping you've caught on to the theme by now! The most important thing you can do is pray. Ask for God's help. When you are at a crossroads and you do not know what to do, pray about it. As you assess your options, ask God for His input.

And remember my challenge for this section: **Do not stress out too much about the decisions you will have to make. As long as you are being motivated by the right things, and as long as you are making it your priority to love God and show His love to others, you will be okay.** You'll never be done navigating through life. Once you graduate or get a job, you will have to decide which person to marry, where to live, which house to buy. The list goes on and on. Finding your way through the many different options life throws at you is an ongoing challenge you will face. I encourage you, though, to ask God for His help and trust there is a larger purpose for you. No matter which direction you go, God will be there with you. How cool is that?

Prayer to reflect on:

When I must make a decision on which direction to go, please guide me, Lord. Help me remember that regardless of which path I take, You will be there with me. Guide me as I assess my options and evaluate what is motivating me. If I am being motivated by the wrong things, help me to reevaluate the reason I am doing what I am doing. Thank you for giving me so many different roads I can travel down. Please guide me as I continue my future endeavors. Amen.

Part Five

Thursday: Finding Relationships

"Bad company corrupts good character." (1 Corinthians 15:33)

If you are anything like I was at the time I left home, you'll leave behind many friendships and relationships. Thanks to social media, it is easier to keep up with old friends. However, part of the joy of leaving home is meeting new people and forming new relationships. Who you spend your time with over the next few years will dramatically impact your future. You will meet so many new people from all walks of life in your upcoming adventure. It's an amazing opportunity, and I challenge you to do as Jesus did and show love to all those you meet.

Just because I am asking you to show love to everyone does not mean I am asking you to actively participate in all the things they do, though. You do not have to agree with what someone does or believes to show love to them. You do not have to approve or support someone's actions to show them love. Simply remember Luke 6:31, which says, "Do to others as you would have them do to you."

In addition to meeting new people, you will undoubtedly be bombarded with a new array of peer pressures from the people you meet. This was made very clear to me in my first week away from home. It was the first

Thursday after I'd fled my parents' nest. I'd been away for almost a week, so I'd become acquainted with many of the other students on campus. At the time, it was common for undergraduates to go out and partake in Iowa City's nightlife on Thursday evenings. Many of my new friends were excited to go experience the downtown atmosphere for the first time. I was excited, too. I was sure it was going to be unlike anything I had ever experienced in the small town where I had been raised. My friends and I spent time getting all dressed up to head out on the town. After an hour or so of going in and out of different venues, it was getting late, and I had class in the morning. It was fun seeing the sights and sounds of the city, but I did not want to miss any of my classes the next day (you can label me a nerd for wanting to get sleep—I am okay with that). I and a few others decided to head home. The other half of the group, though, decided to stay out and pull an "all-nighter." The people in the other group kept asking me to stay out with them. They argued that it was only the first week of classes and that I wouldn't miss much if I slept in. "Come have fun," they said.

Despite the enticing rhetoric they used to persuade me, I decided not to listen to them. I thanked them for the invitation and went home. To this day, I am close friends with those girls who left with me—the girls that had the same priorities I had. I quickly discovered that finding meaningful relationships involves finding people that have similar goals and priorities. I wanted to be open to making new friendships, but I also wanted to stay true to who I was and what I stood for.

Finding meaningful friendships is not always easy. Sometimes, you will want to do what is the more "popular" option, even if it means spending time with people who don't have the same morals, goals, or priorities as you. I promise you, though, that the lasting relationships you make will be the ones with people who have similar priorities, goals, and moral values.

The same goes as you begin to date and experience romantic relationships after you leave home. I have always been an outgoing person, so I went on a variety of dates that first year. At times, I would agree to a date simply because they were a football player or were on track to becoming a medical doctor. These relationships never lasted for more than one or two dates.

You will find, as I did, that it becomes clear pretty quickly if a person has the same priorities, goals, and morals as you. Take my husband, for example. I knew after just a few hours of talking to him that we were on the same page. We had similar interests, similar goals, similar morals, and similar values. While he was not a college athlete and, at the time, was not on track to become a surgeon, I realized that those deeper traits in him were worth hanging onto. Even today, Jeff is still one of the most honest, compassionate, and generous people I know. He puts his relationship with God first. I was able to recognize these traits early on, and that is why I decided to be in a relationship with him.

This brings me to my next challenge for you: **As you seek out new friendships and relationships, I challenge you to not be impressed by the degree someone has, the title they hold, the amount of money they make, or the number of Twitter followers they have. Instead, be impressed by their kindness, their generosity, their integrity, and their ability to show God's love to others.**

Also, remember that first and foremost, the number-one relationship you need to form is your relationship with Jesus. Being Catholic is not just about going to Mass. It is not just about following the Ten Commandments. The most important thing about being Catholic is having a relationship with Jesus. Talk to him as you would talk to a friend. Seek His guidance as you would seek guidance from your most trusted loved one. Ask forgiveness when

> # Challenge # 5
>
> As you seek out new friendships and relationships, I challenge you to not be impressed by the degree someone has, the title they hold, the amount of money they make, or the number of Twitter followers they have. Instead, be impressed by their kindness, their generosity, their integrity, and their ability to show God's love to others.

you have made a mistake. Be open to sharing your thoughts and feelings with Him.

Remember that Jesus's love for you is infinite. It is non-negotiable. He will not stop loving you because you leave a social gathering early to go to bed. He will not stop loving you if you choose the less popular option. He will not even stop loving you if you stop talking to Him. However, as with any relationship, it cannot grow if you do not invest in it.

Make forming a relationship with Jesus your first priority. Instead of only sending up your needs and wants in prayer, try actually talking with Jesus. As you form this relationship, you will find that forming meaningful relationships with other people will become easier, too.

As you begin to navigate new friendships and relationships, please keep these three suggestions in mind:

1. **Work first to form a relationship with Jesus.** As stated above, the most important relationship you can ever form is a relationship with Jesus. How do you do this? The same way you would form any other relationship. Make an effort to talk to Him frequently. Ask forgiveness when you make a mistake. Do more than just vent your problems. Once you have a relationship with Jesus, you will find it becomes easier to keep old friendships and form new ones. As your relationship with Jesus grows, you will grow.

2. **Evaluate the morals and priorities of those around you.** Do not be influenced by the wrong things. Do not be friends with someone or choose to be in a relationship with someone just because of their status, title, or popularity. Choose to surround yourself with people who will build you up—people with similar goals and priorities. These relationships will become the most meaningful to you.

3. **Pray.** Surprise! Of course praying is the most important suggestion I can give you. First, it is impossible to have a growing relationship with Jesus if you do not pray. Second, God is there to help you navigate relationships as you begin to meet new people. Once you

develop friendships and relationships with people you care about, pray for them, too.

Keep in mind my challenge for this week: **As you seek out new friendships and relationships, I challenge you to not be impressed by the degree someone has, the title they hold, the amount of money they make, or the number of Twitter followers they have. Instead, be impressed by their kindness, their generosity, their integrity, and their ability to show God's love to others.** Seek first a relationship with Jesus, and then go from there. Imagine how your life would be if you chose to surround yourself with people who lift you up—with people who challenge you to be a better person.

Prayer to reflect on:

As I begin this new chapter of my life, God, please watch over me as I form new friendships and relationships. Help me remember that money and status is not what I should base my friendships on. I promise I will work to build a relationship with You first. It is my goal to do that before I begin seeking out relationships with other people. You have given me the opportunity to go out and meet new people and form new relationships, and for that I am so grateful. Encourage me to seek out relationships with those who also seek to find a relationship with you. Amen.

Part Six

Friday: Finding Identity

"Do not conform to the pattern of this world, but be transformed by the renewing of your mind. Then you will be able to test and approve what God's will is—His good, pleasing and perfect will." (Romans 12:2)

As I stated before, when you leave home and start a new chapter of your life, you have the awesome opportunity to reevaluate who you want to be—how you define yourself. At this point in your life, you have lived long enough to develop a general understanding of what makes up your identity. As you continue to grow, mature, and take on more responsibility, that identity will undoubtedly grow and mature as well.

It is important to have an understanding of your identity because if we don't know who we are, then we will spend our whole lives looking for the answer. The search for your identity is endless unless you become rooted in finding it with God. Take Adam and Eve, for example. If you read their story in Genesis, you will learn they knew right away that their identity belonged to God. They lost that identity, though, when the evil serpent fooled them into thinking they could find greater meaning for their identity outside of their relationship with God.

You are probably aware that these same evil tactics are used today as a way to dissuade us from looking to God for our identity. The evil tactics may not come from the mouth of a serpent, but they really are everywhere. They trick us into thinking that how we look, what we do, or what titles we hold define our identities.

Here's the good news: Later on in Genesis, God goes looking for Adam and Eve after they have sinned. God does the same for us. Each time we are moved by those evil tactics, God comes looking for us. Yes, your hobbies, interests, and careers do influence who you are. But your identity? That comes from God. Your true identity is knowing that you are a son or daughter of God and that what should define you is the love God gives us and the love we show each other.

Imagine how your image of yourself would change if you simply defined yourself as a loving child of God. What if, instead of using adjectives like tall, short, overweight, athletic, rich, poor, etc., to define your identity, you simply chose to describe yourself as a loving child of God? I am sure the view you have of yourself would be quite different.

It just so happens that I made this same realization in my first week away from home. It was the Friday after I had moved into my new dorm, and we were playing a get-to-know-you activity in one of my classes. The object of the game was to use five adjectives to describe yourself, with one of the adjectives being a "lie." The class then had to then guess which adjective did not describe you.

I thought to myself, "Here is my chance!" From the moment I'd stepped on campus, I'd wondered who I was going to become and what my purpose was going to be. I had started to pray about what God had planned for my life in terms of my purpose and the direction I should take, but I had not thought about what plans God had for me in regards to who I was as a person. Right in that moment, I had the chance to define myself, and I had no idea what I was going to say.

I quickly decided to write down adjectives I was comfortable with. It was just a silly classroom game, right?

In reality, yes, it was just a silly classroom game. However, after I left class that day, I continued to think about how I would define my identity. Who did I want to be? What defined me as a person?

Later on that evening, I thought back to God's purpose for me. My identity and my purpose had to be interconnected, right?

Right. If God's purpose for me is to love Him and show that love to others, then my identity must be simply a loving child of God. Anything beyond that is superfluous.

Yes, today I am a runner. I am a teacher. I am light-hearted and hardworking. I am a wife. A sister. A daughter. And in a few months, I will be a mom.

But all of those titles do not define who I am as a person.

At the end of my life, I want to be known as a person who cared deeply and showed love to everyone around her. Because without that, I cannot serve those other titles.

I cannot be a good wife or daughter or mom without first being a loving child of God.

I cannot be a teacher or an athlete or a friend without first being a loving child of God.

Being a loving child of God comes first. Everything else is a result of that.

And I do not mean to be offensive by calling any young adult or adult a "child." I am simply telling the truth. God is our Father. We will forever be His children—no matter what our age.

So, here is a challenge for you: **As you struggle to define yourself in the coming years, I challenge you to remember that, first and foremost, you are a loving child of God. Every adjective you use to define yourself comes from that.** As you grow and develop, you will find that your interests, hobbies, titles, etc., will change. The adjectives you use to define yourself will grow and evolve. But remember, when we are born into this world, even before becoming a son or

Challenge # 6

As you struggle to define yourself in the coming years, I challenge you to remember that, first and foremost, you are a loving child of God. Every adjective you use to define yourself comes from that.

daughter to our parents, we are God's child. He gave us life, so it is impossible to define our identity without Him. Without Him, we would be nothing.

Just as Adam and Eve faced temptation in Genesis, I am sure you, too, will be tempted by evil tactics to define your identity by means other than your relationship with God. Here are a few suggestions for you to help you resist those evil tactics.

1. **Surround yourself with positive social media.** As a young adult, you are surrounded with all types of social media. Facebook, Twitter, Instagram. The list goes on and on. There are many benefits to social media, but there are also many disadvantages. When we're constantly looking at social media, we end up comparing ourselves to those on the screen. We want to look like them, be as successful as they are, and have as many followers as they do. When we do this, we look to others to define ourselves. This is not okay. Society will tell you to be one thing, while God is telling you to be something entirely different. Do not compare yourself to other people because no one else is like you. Do not let social comparisons ruin your sense of identity and self-worth.

2. **Choose the right role models.** This is very similar to my first suggestion, but it gets a little more specific. We all have role models—people we look up to. Just as you should do when choosing your friends, I encourage you to choose role models that have similar morals and values. Just because a movie star has fame and fortune and beautiful hair or a strong body does not mean you should look to them for guidance on who you should be as a person. When you start looking to the wrong people, another evil tactic gets into your sense of identity.

3. **Pray.** Just as with all the other sections, prayer is essential here. Nobody is perfect. There will be times when social media, peer pressure, society, or a wrong role model will have an effect on you. These evil tactics will replace your identity as a loving child of God with something else. You can, however, seek guidance and forgiveness in prayer. Remember what I said about Adam and Eve? God is always searching for you, just as

he did with Adam and Eve. If you find yourself giving in to an evil tactic, go searching for God. He is already looking for you.

Even when it is difficult to do so, remember my challenge: **As you struggle to define yourself in the coming years, I challenge you to remember that, first and foremost, you are a loving child of God. Every adjective you use to define yourself comes from that.** You cannot be a friend, an athlete, a student, a worker, or anything else without first being a child of God. He gave you life, and everything else comes from that.

Prayer to reflect on:

God, in times when I lose my identity or seek to define it in a way that is not grounded in You, please help me to find my way back. In times when I am influenced by evil tactics like the wrong social media, the wrong role models, or the wrong societal influences, please help me to remember that my identity is with You. I choose to define myself as a loving child of You, God. Help me to remember that, and if I go astray, please help me find my way back to You. Amen.

Part Seven

Today: Finding Your Mission

"He replied, 'Because you have so little faith. Truly I tell you, if you have faith as small as a mustard seed, you can say to this mountain, "Move from here to there," and it will move. Nothing will be impossible for you.'" (Matthew 17:20)

Over the last several parts of this book, we have taken a step back to look at questions about identity and purpose through a different lens. I hope now when you get asked questions about your future plans and your identity, you ask yourself questions like: "Am I answering these questions through conversations I have had with God in prayer?" Or, "Am I answering these questions knowing my identity is first a loving child of God?" Or, "Am I answering these questions knowing that my purpose in life is to love God and show His love to others?" When you start to answer questions about your plans, your identity, or your relationships from the standpoint of being first in a relationship with God, you will find that no matter what you do, you will always feel fulfilled. You will always know who you are.

Think of it this way: Your talents and gifts are gifts God gave you when you were born. He put you where you are for a reason. It is your job to use those talents and gifts the best that you can. Doing anything less than that is simply throwing those gifts away.

The answer to the question of what your purpose is or what your mission is becomes loving God, showing His love to others, and using the gifts He gave you for the greater good.

Think of the Disciples of Jesus. They abandoned any other identity or purpose they had in life other than loving God and showing His love to others. Their mission became spreading that love to others. Over two thousand years later, that mission stays the same.

No, I did not make this discovery in my first week away from home. I did survive that first week, though, and I made it through many years after. I found out I loved school so much that I went on to get a master's degree. Throughout those years, I knew my purpose was to love God and show His love to others, but I never defined it as my *mission*.

The word "mission" is powerful. Your mission is your big goal in life. It is not your career. It is not your title. Your mission is the one thing you want to accomplish. Your mission drives everything else you do. It was not until years later that I realized I wanted my mission in life to be sharing God's love for us all with other people. Honestly, I never really thought about what my *mission* was because I was so focused on my everyday life.

I would like to challenge you to take on this same mission. I am not asking you to go door-to-door preaching about God's love. Rather, I am asking you to be a positive model for others.

Think about what James 1:22-25 says: "Do not merely listen to the word, and so deceive yourselves. Do what it says. Anyone who listens to the word but does not do what it says is like someone who looks at his face in a mirror and, after looking at himself, goes away and immediately forgets what he looks like." Reading the Bible, praying daily, and attending Mass are all excellent ways to continue to build your faith after you leave home. However, if your mission is anything other than actively acting as Jesus would, then it is time for you to reevaluate.

So, here is my last challenge for you: **Help others to grow in their faith. Make it your mission to not only show God's love to others, but to**

help them find their own love in Christ. The ultimate fulfillment is when you see other people following your example. You will feel so fulfilled when you see other people defining themselves as children of God. You will feel fulfilled when you see other people seeking out meaningful relationships as a result of the example you have shown them. You will feel fulfilled when you

> # Challenge # 7
>
> **Help others to grow in their faith. Make it your mission to not only show God's love to others, but to help them find their own love in Christ.**

help other people realize that their biggest purpose in life is to love God and show His love to others.

This may not be an easy thing for you to do. I didn't even figure it out until a few years after graduating from college. Up until that point, I had never even really considered what my mission was.

Here are a few suggestions that may help you get started on your mission:

1. **Be a positive model.** The easiest way to get others to love God and show His love to others is simply to model the positive behavior. Think of what you post on your Facebook, Twitter, or Instagram page. Are those words and pictures modeling the behavior you hope to see in other people? If those words and pictures are not modeling those things, it may be time to reconsider what you're posting. Along those same lines, think about the way you dress, act, and carry yourself. Does what you show on the outside mimic what you are feeling on the inside? These behaviors may not always be what is "popular," but I just ask you to give them a try. I am not asking you to stay in on the weekends, wear turtlenecks everywhere you go, and tattoo a Bible verse to your head. I'm just asking you to make simple changes that will model more positive behavior. You cannot ask other people to love God and show His love to others without first demonstrating both those things with your own actions.

2. **Create a goal, write it down, and stick to it.** Really, the only way to hold yourself accountable for a goal is to actually write it down. I remember, for example, the first time I wanted to sign up to run a marathon. I had always talked about running one in prior years, but until I actually registered myself to run one, I never took the steps necessary to begin training. Take some time to write down what your mission is and what it will take to accomplish it. Are there clubs you would like to join? Mission trips you would like to be part of? Whatever the case, when you write it down, it becomes more real.

3. **Pray.** Again, prayer is the most helpful suggestion I have for you. If your mission is to share God's love with other people, then talking to God will be a big part of that.

Remember my challenge from this section as well: **Help others to grow in their faith. Make it your mission to not only show God's love to others, but to help them find their own love in Christ.**

I hope the sections of this book have challenged you to re-think how you want to approach life when you leave home for the first time. Some of my suggestions may seem more difficult than others, and if you ever begin to feel defeated or lost, reference the verse I included at the top of this last section.

The plant referred to in that verse starts out as a tiny, tiny seed (much like my itty-bitty self as a young freshman). That seed, though, grows up be to around nine feet tall. You are no different than that seed. Imagine how much you can grow if you have faith in yourself and in your relationship with God.

Sure, the next few years may not be filled entirely with smiles and rainbows, but I challenge you to keep perspective and remember the purpose for you being here. When you get defeated or encounter a roadblock, remember that God has a plan for you. Talk to Him about it. Prayer will be the most powerful tool you have.

Remember that God will help you if you help yourself, so surround yourself with good people, make an effort to regularly attend Mass, try your hardest at whatever your put your mind to, and use the gifts God has given you to their fullest potential.

Prayer to reflect on:

I am making it my mission in life to show Your love to other people, God. I hope to do this by being a positive model for those around me. I will love others like You love me, and as a result, I hope to make the world around me a better place. I feel ready to begin my journey away from home as long as I have Your guidance and support, God. Thank you for this opportunity You have given me to leave home and grow on my own. Amen.

CPSIA information can be obtained
at www.ICGtesting.com
Printed in the USA
LVHW030427140519
617701LV00002B/2/P